RICHARD BONG

Other Badger Biographies

Belle and Bob La Follette: Partners in Politics
Caroline Quarlls and the Underground Railroad
Casper Jaggi: Master Swiss Cheese Maker
Curly Lambeau: Building the Green Bay Packers
Dr. Kate: Angel on Snowshoes
Harley and the Davidsons: Motorcycle Legends
Mai Ya's Long Journey
Mountain Wolf Woman: A Ho-Chunk Girlhood
Ole Evinrude and His Outboard Motor
A Recipe for Success: Lizzie Kander and Her Cookbook
Tents, Tigers, and the Ringling Brothers

RICHARD BONG
★ World War II Flying Ace ★

Pete Barnes

Wisconsin Historical Society Press

Published by the Wisconsin Historical Society Press
Publishers since 1855

© 2009 by State Historical Society of Wisconsin

For permission to reuse material from *Richard Bong: World War II Flying Ace* (ISBN 978-0-87020-434-0), please access www.copyright.com or contact the Copyright Clearance Center, Inc. (CCC), 222 Rosewood Drive, Danvers, MA 01923, 978-750-8400. CCC is a not-for-profit organization that provides licenses and registration for a variety of users.

wisconsin**history**.org

Photographs identified with WHi or WHS are from the Society's collections; address requests to reproduce these photos to the Visual Materials Archivist at the Wisconsin Historical Society, 816 State Street, Madison, WI 53706. Unless otherwise noted, all other images are property of the Richard I. Bong Veterans Historical Center. Please direct inquiries about such photos to the Curator at the Richard I. Bong Veterans Historical Center, 305 Harborview Parkway, Superior, WI 54880.

Printed in Wisconsin, U.S.A.
Designed by Jill Bremigan

13 12 11 10 09   1 2 3 4 5

Library of Congress Cataloging-in-Publication Data

Barnes, Pete.
  Richard Bong : World War II flying ace / Pete Barnes.
      p. cm.—(Badger biographies)
  Includes bibliographical references and index.
  ISBN 978-0-87020-434-0 (pbk. : alk. paper) 1. Bong, Richard I—Juvenile literature. 2. United States. Army Air Forces—Biography—Juvenile literature. 3. Fighter pilots—United States—Biography—Juvenile literature. 4. World War, 1939-1945—Aerial operations, American—Juvenile literature. 5. World War, 1939-1945—Pacific Area—Juvenile literature. I. Title.
  UG626.2.B66B376 2009
  940.54'4973092—dc22
  [B]

                              2009000991

Front and back cover images courtesy of the Richard I. Bong Veterans Historical Center.

∞ The paper used in this publication meets the minimum requirements of the American National Standard for Information Sciences—Permanence of Paper for Printed Library Materials, ANSI Z39.48-1992.

To Sophia, the most important girl in my life

Publication of this book was made possible, in part, by gifts
from Richard Grum and Mrs. Harvey E. Vick of Milwaukee, Wisconsin.
Additional funding was provided by a grant from the
D. C. Everest fellowship fund.

Contents

1 Sky-High Dreams 1

2 Learning to Fly 11

3 Off to War 28

4 The Fight for New Guinea 41

5 A Reluctant Hero Comes Home 53

6 Ace of Aces 65

7 Home for Good 75

   Appendix: Richard's Time Line 95

   Glossary 97

   Reading Group Guide and Activities 105

   To Learn More about Richard Bong

      and World War II 107

   Acknowledgments 108

   Index 109

1

Sky-High Dreams

On a hot day in August 1945, a long, black car drove slowly down the dirt road leading from the Bong family farm to the small cemetery in nearby Poplar, Wisconsin. Thousands of people lined the road, heads bowed in respect for a fallen American hero. Farmers and storekeepers, schoolchildren and grandmothers—they had all come to say good-bye to Major Richard Bong. The people of Poplar had cheered him when he returned from World War II just a few months before. Bong was America's most successful **flying ace**, a fighter pilot who had protected the skies of the **South Pacific** from Japanese attack. Now they **mourned** his death in a tragic flying accident. Few would forget his bravery in **combat** or his **commitment** to the difficult task of defeating the Japanese empire and bringing peace to the world.

flying ace: a highly skilled military pilot   **South Pacific**: area south of the equator that includes Australia, New Guinea, and the East Indies   **mourned** (mornd): felt sadness or grief for someone who has died
combat: fighting between people or armies   **commitment**: promise to do something or support something

1

By 1945, World War II had dragged on for 5 long years. More than 70 million people on both sides had lost their lives. Not just soldiers, but women and children had died by the millions during bombing attacks and other **assaults** on cities all over Europe and Asia. Richard Bong was just one of many young Americans who left home to fight in the war. Like thousands of others, he wanted to help America and its **allies** preserve freedom. As his funeral car rolled slowly along, the people of Poplar thought about the loss of such a special American, a man who had known since childhood he would make his mark on the world high up in the skies.

The year was 1928. Young Richard froze and looked up to the sky, a fishing pole balanced on his left shoulder. He listened carefully to the faraway drone of the army airplane delivering mail to President Calvin Coolidge. President Coolidge was on vacation nearby, on Cedar Island in Lake **Superior**. All thoughts of fishing in the creek were forgotten as Richard imagined himself in the **cockpit**, **confidently** guiding

assault (uh **sawlt**): violent attack on someone or something   **ally** (**al** I): friend, especially during wartime
Superior: su **pir** ee ur   **cockpit**: the area in the front of a plane where the pilot sits   **confidently**: with a strong belief in your own abilities

2

the plane through the clouds. Little did he know that years later he would become America's most highly honored pilot.

Richard was an excellent student at Superior Central High School.

Richard's younger sister Jerry ended his daydream. "Richard, come on!" she insisted. "We've only got a couple of hours before we have to be back for evening chores." Richard turned and followed his sisters down the path toward the creek. He would have time later that night to work on his newest model airplane and dream of his future as a pilot.

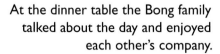

At the dinner table the Bong family talked about the day and enjoyed each other's company.

There was never much time for daydreaming on the Bong family farm in Poplar, a tiny town of just 500 people in the northwest corner of Wisconsin. It's not that there weren't enough people around to do the work. It's just that there was always something to do. Richard was the oldest of 8 children. They all helped milk the cows, feed the pigs and chickens, and work in the fields around the farm. As the oldest son, Richard had lots of responsibilities. His father, Carl, worked on road **construction** most days, so Richard was in charge of keeping the farm going. He was usually awake at 5:00 in the morning and working hard until the school bus came.

WHI IMAGE ID 62124

WHI IMAGE ID 50980

Small family farms were common when Richard Bong was growing up.

Many farms had a tractor for plowing fields.

construction: building something large, like a house, road, or bridge

4

Richard's favorite chore was **tilling** the soil using his father's 1936 Caterpillar tractor. The Caterpillar was tricky to operate—heavy and difficult to steer—but Richard made it look easy. He could plow an **acre** in an hour and loved pushing the tractor into sharp turns at the end of each row. The arm strength and **hand-eye coordination** he gained from all of those hours plowing fields later made pushing an airplane into dives and rolls much easier.

When work was finished, the Bong family looked for fun. In the fall, all of the men and older boys went deer hunting or trout fishing on the **Brule** River. When winter came, the children ice-skated on the frozen river. During the summer, they played

Richard and his father loved hunting deer for the family dinner table.

tilling: preparing land for growing crops   **acre** (ay kur): an area almost as large as a football field, or 43,560 square feet   **hand-eye coordination** (koh ord uhn ay shun): using the eyes to direct the hands, as in handwriting or baseball   **Brule**: brool

5

golf on a small course they built in the clearing behind their house. Even though they were far from other families, it was rarely quiet around the Bong household.

Richard stayed busier than anyone else in the family. After school he could often be found playing baseball or basketball. He was short but athletic, with a mean curveball and a quick jump shot. He liked almost every sport and was well liked by teammates because he played hard but fair.

Richard also played **clarinet** in the school band and sang in the church choir. Even his mother admitted he was "not much of a clarinet player," but he sang beautifully. Years later Richard belted out his favorite tunes while zooming through the skies in his P-38 Lightning airplane. He was active with the **4-H Club** and planted a row of evergreen trees on the family property as his final project.

Richard looked like a young soldier in his band uniform.

clarinet (klair uh **net**): a woodwind instrument shaped like a long, straight tube with a small horn on the end
4-H Club: a club where kids learn farming and home economics

Generally a quiet and polite person, Richard had another side seen by only his family and close friends. He had teasing nicknames for his brothers and sisters: Joyce was "Knock-knees," his sisters Jerry and Nel were "Monkey-face" and "Fats," and his brother Bud was called "Buckshot." He also **tormented** family and friends with practical jokes. When Richard and his friend Peter wanted to play a trick on their friend Tony, they suggested a contest to see who could jump the deepest into a huge pile of snow near the Bong family farm. Tony agreed to go first and leaped into the snow up to his neck. Richard and Peter quickly ran away, laughing loudly as Tony cried for help. Eventually, they came back and dug him out.

Despite his **hectic** schedule, Richard was an excellent student. He balanced all of his interests and responsibilities with his endless energy and enthusiasm for life. He graduated from high school in 1938 number 14 out of a class of 400.

Many people thought that because Richard was the oldest son, he would take over the family farm. But Richard had other plans. Even though he loved driving his father's Caterpillar tractor, he knew his future lay not on a farm but up in the sky.

tormented: upset or annoyed someone on purpose   hectic: very busy

His dream was to be a pilot. This meant he needed to go to college for at least 2½ years before he could enter the United States **Army Air Corps**. Richard finished high school in 1938 and immediately enrolled at Superior State Teachers College just 15 miles from Poplar. Not ready to **abandon** his family, Richard lived at home and helped with the morning chores before driving to classes each day. This commitment to hard work later made him one of the most successful air force pilots in American history.

Just a year after Richard graduated from high school, World War II broke out in Europe and Asia. This war happened after years of **conflict** between Germany, Italy, and Japan and their neighbors. Several countries had powerful **dictators**. In Germany, Adolph Hitler's powerful army stormed across Europe and North Africa with the help of Italy's dictator, **Benito Mussolini**. Japanese armies led by General **Hideki Tōjō** marched across China and other parts of the Asian continent. These 3 dictators and their armies were known as the Axis powers. They were opposed by the British, Russians,

Army Air Corps (cor): the aircraft service of the army, before the air force was started
abandon (uh **ban** duhn): leave forever   **conflict**: difference and disagreement   **dictator** (**dik** tay tur): a leader who has absolute power over his country   **Benito Mussolini**: buh **nee** toh moo suh **lee** nee
Hideki Tōjō: hee de kee toh joh

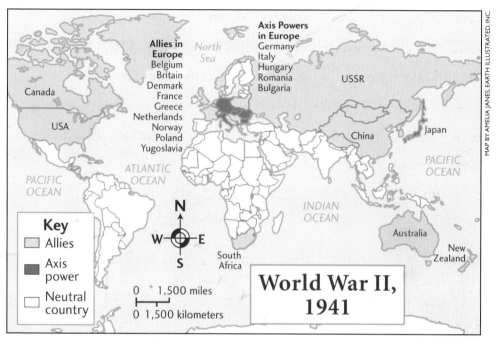

Allies in Europe
Belgium
Britain
Denmark
France
Greece
Netherlands
Norway
Poland
Yugoslavia

Axis Powers in Europe
Germany
Italy
Hungary
Romania
Bulgaria

North Sea

USSR

Canada

USA

China

Japan

ATLANTIC OCEAN

PACIFIC OCEAN

PACIFIC OCEAN

INDIAN OCEAN

Australia

New Zealand

South Africa

Key
Allies
Axis power
Neutral country

N
W — E
S

0   1,500 miles
0 1,500 kilometers

World War II, 1941

MAP BY AMELIA JANES, EARTH ILLUSTRATED, INC.

World War II spread across the globe as the Axis powers gained land and power.

Chinese, and other countries known as the Allied forces. The
Axis powers wanted power, **natural resources** such as oil
and metals, and more land. Axis leaders and governments
threatened freedom all around the world. Their armies
imprisoned and killed millions of people. Many people lost
their lives fighting against the Axis powers.

natural resource: a commonly used material that comes from the earth, such as oil, coal, or iron

Many people in the United States did not want to join the war. Americans helped Great Britain and the Allies by sending supplies, ships, and weapons across the Atlantic. But the United States did not officially join the war until December of 1941. That's when the Japanese attacked the American naval base at Pearl Harbor.

2

Learning to Fly

Becoming a pilot was difficult and dangerous. When Richard enlisted in the Army Air Force as a flying **cadet** in May of 1941, he knew the odds were against his ever getting flyer's wings. More than half of the men wishing to be pilots "**washed out**" or failed the checkup and written tests required to start the program. To be a pilot, you even had to have perfect eyesight! Most who failed were sent to the **infantry**, where they would fight from the ground. But Richard passed all of the tests with flying colors.

Even so, learning to fly was dangerous. Many who passed the tests were hurt or killed in training accidents or failed to master one of the many skills required to fly. The program required at least 200 hours of flying to become an official pilot. That meant many days and nights of takeoffs and landings, **navigation** practice, night flying, and other difficult tasks.

cadet (kuh **det**): a young person training to become a member of the armed forces   **washed out**: failed
infantry (**in** fuhn tree): the part of the army that fights on foot   **navigation**: the science of directing an aircraft

11

Just one mistake meant being kicked out of the program, or worse: injury or death. For this dangerous work, cadets were paid only $2.50 a day plus a free room, food, and basic supplies.

Richard's first stop for flight training was in **Tulare**, California. This meant his first trip across country, more than 1,500 miles from home. As Richard got on the bus for his long trip, his father gave him some simple advice: "Do as you are told, do your best, and you will do fine." Richard would remember these words as he traveled around the world to defend his country and follow his dreams.

WHI IMAGE ID 43590

The trip from Wisconsin to California was a long and **eventful** one. His first stop was in Chicago, where he switched from the bus to a train that carried him west. Richard was amazed by the

Trains carried soldiers like this one to military bases all over the United States.

Tulare: too **lair** ee   **eventful:** filled with things that are interesting or important

12

large crowds and constant **din** of Chicago. "It is so noisy you can hardly hear yourself think," he said of the city. He liked Chicago better after dark, especially because "at night the town is actually brighter than in daytime."

Richard was less impressed with the crowded train and its tiny beds. Two cadets squeezed onto each bunk. That meant they had to stay close together, or, as Richard remembered, "the one on the outside wall will fall into the aisle." The cadets sat for many hours watching the countryside roll by and trading stories about their hometowns. All of them were glad to finally get off the train and start their training.

Richard and his new friends quickly learned that life was tough for first-year cadets. New cadets were called "**dodos**" and were expected to follow all the orders given by **upperclassmen**. When an upperclassman called out "Red light!" all the dodos had to freeze until they heard "Green light!"

din: great deal of noise   dodo (doh doh): first-year flying school cadet   upperclassman: student who has finished the first year in a training program or school

Training planes like the AT-11 were easier to fly than combat planes.

Dodos were also given **demerits** for breaking rules. Upperclassmen gave demerits any time a dodo broke a rule. If their uniforms were not perfectly ironed, if they were late to morning exercises, or even if they forgot an important word about flying, they were given a demerit. Six or more demerits, and dodos could not go to town for a night off on

demerit (di **mair** it): a mark made against one's record

14

the weekend. Every demerit over 8 meant an hour of walking around the **military base**. One cadet got 20 demerits and was forced to walk around the base for 12 hours straight!

Nearly every minute of a cadet's life was spent doing some kind of training. Cadets awoke at 5:30, dressed and cleaned their rooms, and then reported for morning exercises at

exactly 6:20. They had only 5 minutes to change out of their exercise clothes, wash and comb their hair, and get to the **mess hall** for breakfast. They marched into the dining hall and then sat silently until the officer commanded them to turn over their plates and eat. The rest of the day was completely filled with classes, athletic **drills**, and flying practice. When they

IMAGE COURTESY OF THE LIBRARY OF CONGRESS

Army Air Force cadets trained long and hard to prepare for war.

military base: an area owned by the government, used to train soldiers and store weapons
mess hall: dining hall on a military base   **drill**: lesson on how to do something by doing it over and over again

15

weren't learning something, the cadets were marching in straight lines around the base. When lights went out at 10:00 p.m., Richard and his classmates were often too exhausted to talk.

Although marching in the 100-degree California sun was rough, **academic** classes were often the most tiring part of a cadet's day. In order to use an airplane's **instruments** and learn the basics of flight, cadets had to first master **algebra** and **trigonometry**. They also learned how to use a **slide rule**, how airplane engines worked, and how the weather affected an airplane's flight. Some cadets who were in great physical shape washed out of the flight program because they could not handle these difficult classes.

This cadet uses detailed maps to plot a course through unfamiliar skies.

academic (ak uh **dem** ik): having to do with school   **instrument**: tool used in navigating flight
algebra (**al** juh bruh): mathematics that uses letters and symbols to represent numbers in equations
trigonometry (trig uh **nom** uh tree): a type of mathematics that deals with angles and triangles
slide rule: a ruler with a sliding piece used for making calculations before calculators were invented

IMAGE COURTESY OF THE NATIONAL
MUSEUM OF THE U.S. AIR FORCE

Flying planes for the Army Air Force was challenging
work, but also lots of fun.

Luckily, not everything about flight training was difficult. Richard quickly made good friends with many of his **fellow** cadets. They bragged about their mothers' home cooking and laughed about the crazy things they were required to do, like being forced to wear goggles when eating grapefruit to protect their eyes from spraying juice. Richard saw the Pacific Ocean for the first time and marveled at the sunny weather that seemed to exist all year long in California.

Best of all, flying was even more fun than Richard had imagined. He loved pushing his airplane through all kinds of acrobatic **maneuvers**. By turning the control wheel sharply to the left or right, Richard could turn the plane upside down and then roll it back upright again. By pulling back on the wheel

fellow: in the same group, or with the same rank   **maneuver** (muh **noo** vur): difficult movement that needs planning and skill

17

he could bring the plane's nose high into the air until it looped over backward. If he was high enough, he could push the wheel forward and the plane would dive quickly toward the ground.

All of these maneuvers were challenging to perform correctly. Even so, Richard complained that it was too easy. He said he was "so used to steep turns and upside down flying that I don't get a thrill out of it anymore." He also had to get used to "blacking out" while flying, a common event for fighter pilots. He later recalled, "I've blacked myself out a couple of times diving out of a half roll. The reason is that I roll the plane over on its back and hang there for a minute or more and the blood rushes to my head. Then I dive the plane and come right side up and the pressure causes me to black out. Everything turns black and I can't see a thing for a few seconds."

Despite the excitement of learning to fly, Richard often felt homesick. He wrote his mother nearly every day, giving updates on his training and asking about life on the Bong family farm. He also sent his parents money when he could. He knew how badly his help was missed on the farm.

In August of 1941, Richard and the other cadets completed the first stage of flight training. At graduation, their **instructor** Tex Rankin put on an **air show** to celebrate, running his plane through dozens of **aerial** maneuvers. He even wrote the numbers "1941" in the sky!

But that was just the first part of training. The cadets were soon at their next training station, Gardner Field in Taft, California. No longer dodos, the cadets didn't have to fear the constant **badgering** of upperclassmen or worry about losing their weekend passes because of too many demerits. What they did do was fly—a lot. Their new training plane was called the Basic Trainer 13-A, a solidly built, slow plane made for simple flying. Cadets were expected to know this airplane inside and out and to master flying it in all sorts of weather.

One of the most difficult tasks to master at Gardner Field was flying at night. Cadets learned to fly using only their instruments, because they could not see landmarks such as rivers or mountains to tell where they were. Richard quickly mastered the skills involved, although night flying made him nervous. "You get a funny feeling when you're sitting in that

instructor: teacher   air show: demonstration of airplane maneuvers for a crowd   aerial (air ee uhl): in the air
badgering (badj ur ing): continually asking someone to do something

airplane and you can't see the ground," he said. "It seems like I'm turning to the right when I'm going straight ahead."

Four F4U Corsairs fly in tight formation over the Pacific Ocean.

Cadets also learned to fly in **formation** with just a few feet between each airplane. Often 8 or 10 planes flew together in tight "V" patterns, like a flock of geese. This was a common method used to keep airplanes together during combat **missions**. If one pilot made a small mistake and bumped into his neighbor's wing, both airplanes could spin out of control and crash. Pilots had to remain focused at all times and constantly check to see where the other planes were around them.

Cadets formed close friendships during their many hours together.

formation: a special arrangement of planes in the air   mission: in war, an assignment to capture, defend, or destroy

Richard learned the importance of staying alert after surviving an accident at the end of a training flight. As his plane landed he did not slow down fast enough, and he clipped the wing of an airplane stopped at the end of the runway. Richard's plane tilted violently to one side and spun off of the runway into a ditch. The propeller dug noisily into the ground, and one of the wings was badly damaged. Fortunately, no one was hurt. Richard's trainers did not consider his mistake serious enough to kick him out of the program—but it certainly was a wake-up call for him!

Learning to fly was often quite stressful. Richard and his fellow cadets escaped the stress by enjoying the sights of California. Richard was not very impressed with the Pacific Ocean, however. "I saw the ocean but it isn't very inspiring," he wrote his mother. "It looks like Lake Superior." He was more excited about a football game he saw between the University of Southern California and the University of Wisconsin. In Superior, football was usually played in the bitter cold, but in sunny California he could watch football in a short-sleeved shirt.

By November of 1941, Richard and his fellow cadets were ready to move on to the final stage, advanced flight training at Luke Field in **Phoenix**, Arizona. Little did they know that just one month later the Japanese would attack the American naval base at Pearl Harbor and the United States would enter World War II.

Very early in the morning on December 7, 1941, 350 Japanese **fighter and bomber planes** attacked the U.S. naval base at Pearl Harbor, Hawaii. The attack was a complete surprise. Five American warships were sunk, and many more were damaged during the attack. Nearly 200 U.S. fighter planes were also destroyed, most of them before they ever made it off the ground. Worst of all, more than 2,400 people were killed, and more than 1,200 were wounded. They weren't just soldiers. They were doctors, nurses, and people who weren't even in the military. The United States had never been attacked in such a **brutal** manner before, and people across the country were shocked by the news. America had tried to stay out of World War II, but the very next day President Franklin **Roosevelt** asked **Congress** to declare war on Japan. A few days later, Germany,

Phoenix: fee niks   **fighter plane**: a plane whose main job is to attack other planes   **bomber plane**: a plane whose main job is to drop bombs on targets on land or sea   **brutal**: extremely violent   **Roosevelt: roh** zuh velt
Congress: the part of American government where laws and other important decisions are made

The Japanese attack on Pearl Harbor shocked and angered Americans.

Japan's ally, declared war on the United States. This forced America to enter World War II in Europe.

Richard was ready to fight. His skills as a pilot were top-notch. Many of the cadets considered Richard the best flyer at Luke Field. When an experienced army pilot arrived at

Luke with the new **Lockheed** P-38 Lightning fighter plane,
Richard's friends set up a flying contest between the 2 pilots.
The P-38 was faster than Richard's AT-6 training plane, so many
of those watching expected him to lose. Just the opposite
happened. The Lightning's pilot tried all sorts of maneuvers—
spins, steep dives, and sharp turns. No matter what he tried,
Richard's plane ended up right behind him, in an easy position
to shoot him down. There was no question that Richard Bong
was one of the most gifted pilots in the Army Air Force.

Like most pilots, Richard wanted to **serve** his country. After
Pearl Harbor he and his friends spent many hours talking

about the war
and imagining
what their part
would be. After
graduation in
January, many of
the pilots were
stationed at fighter
training bases.

The P-38 Lightning was a fast and powerful fighter plane.

Lockheed: an airplane company that built many planes for the U.S. military   **serve**: to work, especially for the military, the church, or one's country   **stationed**: sent to a particular military base

They quickly moved on to combat jobs in Europe or in the Pacific. Not Richard. He was asked to stay at Luke Field and serve as a flight instructor for new cadets.

At first Richard was disappointed. He had gone through training to become a combat pilot, not to teach others how to fly. Instead of moping around, however, he quickly decided to make the best of it. At least he was still flying, and the extra practice would make him more ready if he ever made it into combat. Besides, he was still serving his country by helping other young pilots become top-notch flyers. His time for combat would come soon enough.

Richard quickly learned that instructing other pilots was even more difficult than learning to fly himself. He had struggled to fly at night and to stay in tight air formations, but to teach pilots in training to do these things was a true challenge. Richard wrote his mother, "The fastest way to recognize your own weaknesses is to try to teach someone else." His greatest fear was that one of his students would get hurt or be killed because he failed as a teacher.

None of Richard's cadets died, but many other student pilots did lose their lives. One awful night, 5 airplanes and 4 cadets were lost during a terrible crash. Richard loved the danger and excitement of flying, but accidents such as these made him realize how close he was to death every time he stepped into an airplane.

Richard enjoyed the beauty of the Grand Canyon from his training plane.

Despite the constant dangers, Richard could not resist the urge to push his flying skills to the limit. He loved "hedge-hopping" at 100 feet above the ground on search missions, the treetops flashing past at 300 miles per hour. Instead of simply enjoying the beauty of the Grand Canyon while flying overhead, he flew inside its walls and turned loops. Although he was a quiet person on the ground, his wild side came alive in the sky.

Richard's job as an instructor ended suddenly in May 1942. That's when he was told to go to Hamilton Field near San Francisco, California. There, he would go through fighter training to prepare for **duty**. Richard was excited at the chance to fight. Just as he predicted, in only a few short months his career as a fighter pilot in the South Pacific would begin.

duty: period of service in war

3

Off to War

For Richard Bong, the best part of combat fighter training was leaving behind the clunky and slow training planes he flew as a cadet. It was time for the real thing, the new Lockheed P-38 Lightning. The P-38 was bigger, faster, and more powerful than any plane Richard had flown before. He fell in love with it immediately. "Wooey! What an airplane," he wrote home. "That's all I can say, but that is enough."

Richard loved flying the P-38 Lightning.

Not everyone had such kind words for the P-38. Much bigger than its cousins the P-39 and P-40, the P-38 looked more like a small bomber,

28

loaded with heavy bombs, than a fighter plane. With huge
1,000-**horsepower** engines and protective armor, it weighed
more than 15,000 pounds. That's as much as the weight of 5
cars! The "P" in P-38 stood for "pursuit" plane, which meant it
was a plane that chased enemy planes in order to shoot them
down. But some people felt the P-38 was too **cumbersome**
to perform well against the **agile** Japanese fighter planes.
The quick-turning Japanese Zero and other combat planes

had already shot
down hundreds of
American planes
over the Pacific.
Some people feared
the P-38 would meet
the same fate. But
they would soon be
proven wrong.

You could tell a Japanese Zero by the "O" on its side.

With a top speed of 395 miles per hour, the P-38 was one
of the fastest American planes in the war. It could climb to an
incredible 39,000 feet. From there it could launch surprise

horsepower: a unit of power equal to the power of one horse   cumbersome (**kuhm** bur suhm): clumsy and
heavy   **agile** (**aj** uhl): able to move quickly and easily

attacks on enemy pilots who couldn't see it so high above them. Four **.50-caliber** machine guns and a powerful **20 mm cannon** were buried in the plane's nose. These guns made sure that enemy planes could not escape a direct hit. Having twin engines meant the P-38 could fly longer distances than other fighters, because they needed only one engine to fly. When one engine was damaged, the plane could still return to base. Pilots quickly learned to overcome the P-38's slow turning abilities by diving down on enemy planes and speeding away. The agile Japanese fighter planes would soon be challenged.

Four machine guns poke out of this P-38's nose.

.50-caliber: gun with a half-inch barrel   **20 mm (millimeter) cannon**: gun with a 20 millimeter barrel

Early in the war, Japanese and German airplanes ruled the skies. Their pilots were excellent, and their planes were as good as anything the Allies flew. But after America joined the war, American planes were clearly better. By 1943, U.S. Navy planes such as the F6F Hellcat and the F4U Corsair were knocking Japanese Zeros out of the sky. Army Air Force planes such as the P-38 Lightning and the P-47 Thunderbolt were

The F4U Corsair was a favorite among American pilots.

Many consider the P-51 Mustang America's greatest fighter plane.

also successful. America's greatest fighter plane was probably the P-51 Mustang. It was fast, powerful, and able to fly from Chicago to Los Angeles without refueling. American factories

31

produced these planes in record numbers. In 1944, the United States produced more airplanes than all of those made by the Japanese and Germans.

At Hamilton Field, Richard and his fellow combat pilots learned to love the power and speed of their new planes. Richard thought the P-38 was easy to fly. He spent many hours learning combat maneuvers, shooting at targets in the air and on the ground, and learning his way around the skies above San Francisco. When not in the air he had little to do but relax and enjoy himself. "All I do around here is go bowling and play ping-pong and sleep when I'm not flying," he reported to his mother.

Just when it looked as though Richard would soon be leaving the United States for his first combat post, he was **grounded** for making a flight that wasn't allowed. One of his friends had just been married and lived close to the air base in **San Anselino**. To celebrate, Richard **buzzed** low over his friend's house. Neighbors scattered in fear at the roar of the low-flying plane. One woman called the base, complaining that her laundry had been blown from the clothesline and

grounded: not allowed to fly   **San Anselino**: san an suh **lee** noh   **buzzed**: in an airplane, flew low to the ground

that she had spilled her dinner all over the kitchen as she dove for cover. Richard's **commanding officer**, **General** George Kenney, was furious.

Richard could have been kicked out of the Army Air Force because of his stunt. Flying low over people's homes was a serious offense. Luckily for Richard, several other pilots were caught playing similar tricks. His friend Bob **O'Neill** and 2 others were busted for flying underneath the Golden Gate Bridge on that same day.

Only a very bold pilot would attempt to fly underneath the Golden Gate Bridge.

The Army Air Force needed talented pilots. Few officers wanted to lose men like Richard Bong because of one mistake. Richard was also lucky that General Kenney liked him. Kenney was commander of the Fifth Air Force. He was busy planning for a base in New **Guinea** where 50 P-38s would join a group of P-40 Warhawks and P-47 Thunderbolts. It would be their job to defend Australia and the South

commanding officer officer in charge of a military unit   **General**: the person with the highest rank in the U.S. army   **O'Neill**: oh **neel**   **Guinea**: **gin** ee

Pacific from Japanese attack. General Kenney knew Richard's reputation as a talented pilot and a good person. Richard was just the type of pilot Kenney needed for his new attack force. He didn't want to send Richard home, but he planned to give him a good scare to teach him a lesson.

General George Kenney of the Fifth Air Force.

General Kenney called Richard into his office and yelled at him for taking risks with his airplane. He reminded Richard of the thousands of soldiers dying in the war and accused him of not taking his job seriously. Kenney's voice grew louder and louder. The quiet farm boy stood, nervously awaiting his fate. He expected the general to demand his pilot's wings and to send him back to Wisconsin. Instead, Kenney reminded him that he was a busy man and did not like receiving phone calls about his pilots' bad behavior. Richard would have to write a 5,000-word paper on safe flying and read it to the entire **squadron**. He would be grounded for 6 weeks. Finally, he would report to the woman whose laundry he had ruined and help her with chores for a day.

squadron: a unit of between 12 and 24 pilots

34

Richard felt a huge sense of relief. Six weeks was a long time to go without flying, but it was a lot better than being kicked out of the Army Air Force. Richard promised not to make the same mistake again and quickly left Kenney's office. But he would be seeing more of General Kenney in just a few months.

Military Ranks

Military ranks tell us the order of power. You can tell a person's rank by the symbol—like a star or a leaf—on his or her uniform. Generals are at the top, and cadets are at the bottom. From the top down, the order of military rank is

General

General

Brigadier General

Colonel

Lieutenant Colonel

Major

Captain

Lieutenant

Lieutenant Colonel

Cadet

The higher the rank, the more soldiers the officer commands. For example, a lieutenant is usually in charge of about 50 soldiers. While in the Army Air Force, Richard Bong moved all the way from cadet to major.

Lieutenant Colonel: loo **ten** uhnt **kur** nuhl

As Richard counted the days until he could fly again, World War II raged on in 60 different countries around the globe. The German **blitzkrieg**, or "lightning war," had forced much of Europe into **Nazi** hands. Poland, Denmark, Belgium, France, and many other countries could not defend themselves from the heavy air attacks from the German **Luftwaffe** air force or stop German tanks from rolling across their borders. The American military had joined the British and the Russians in the fight against the Nazis after Pearl Harbor, but Hitler's army was a powerful enemy.

IMAGE COURTESY OF THE PATTON MUSEUM OF CAVALRY AND ARMOR

German tanks swept across Europe early in the war.

In the east, Japan continued to control the entire Pacific region. American troops in the Pacific were led by General Douglas MacArthur. MacArthur was forced to abandon the **Philippines** when more than 2 million Japanese soldiers defeated the 130,000 Americans

blitzkrieg (blits kreeg): German for "lightning war," because of how quickly it moved   **Nazi** (nah tsee): a brutal political party in Germany from 1933–1945 that was led by Adolf Hitler   **Luftwaffe: luft** vah fuh   **Philippines: fil** uh peenz

stationed in the area. Like Germany, Japan had taken control of many of the countries closest to it: **Thailand**, **Guam**, Burma, and **Borneo**. Now it was threatening Australia. A Japanese submarine even fired shells at the California coast, the first attack on American soil since the War of 1812.

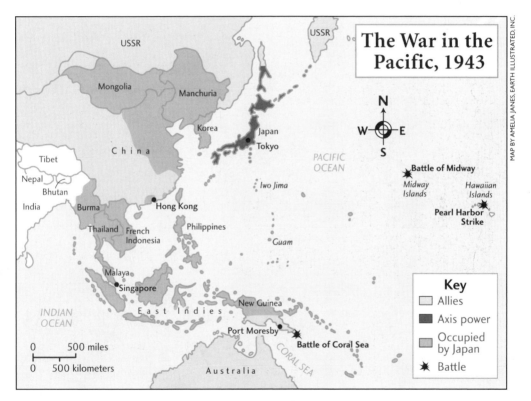

The war for control in the Pacific was long and fierce.

Thailand: tI land   **Guam**: gwahm   **Borneo**: bor nee oh

37

The Americans soon began fighting back. Lieutenant Colonel James Doolittle led a group of B-25 Mitchell bombers in a surprise attack on Tokyo in April of 1942. The attack shocked the enemy and encouraged many frightened Americans. That May, the American and British navies were

The Japanese did not think the Americans would be so powerful in the air.

able to push Japan back from New Guinea and Australia at the Battle of Coral Sea. Still confident it could crush the U.S. Navy, the Japanese navy attacked the U.S. base at Midway Island just a month later. But Japan's luck had changed for the worse. When the Americans decoded Japanese radio messages and discovered the Japanese battle **strategy**, American **dive-bombers** launched a **counterattack** that destroyed 4 Japanese aircraft carriers, 300 planes, and more than 3,500 men.

After this defeat the Japanese only fought harder. The Japanese were proud of their nation. Their desire to serve Emperor Hirohito, the Japanese leader, made many Japanese soldiers fight to the death. Japanese soldiers often blew themselves up with hand grenades rather than become prisoners. Japanese pilots nicknamed "**kamikaze**" purposely crashed their planes

IMAGE COURTESY OF THE LIBRARY OF CONGRESS

Even after terrible defeats the Japanese refused to surrender.

strategy (**strat** uh jee): plan for achieving a specific goal   **dive-bomber**: an airplane that drops its bombs while diving at the enemy   **counterattack**: an attack in reply to an attack   **kamikaze** (kah mi **kah** zee): Japanese pilot who kills himself in battle

39

into American warships. The struggle in the Pacific would last 3 more years and cost millions of more lives before it ended.

General Kenney finally received the promised 50 P-38 Lightnings in September of 1942. Richard Bong was one of the first pilots he chose to fly these powerful planes. Richard was excited at the news and immediately began getting ready for his departure. He wrote a short letter to his mom before boarding the transport plane to New Guinea. In the letter he predicted his own future: "I won't see home until the war is over, unless I get over there and become a hero so they send me home for a couple months."

Richard did become a war hero and was sent home twice by his officers in recognition of all he had done. But first he would face hundreds of hours in fierce combat and survive many close calls with death.

4

The Fight for New Guinea

Poplar, Wisconsin, and Port **Moresby**, New Guinea, are as different as two places can be. Richard spent his first nights in camp near Port Moresby dreaming about the cool winds off Lake Superior, deer hunting in the winter woods, and sitting down with his family to plates of fried chicken and farm vegetables. Many times his dreams were interrupted by the drone of "Washing Machine Charley," a noisy old bomber the Japanese sent at nighttime to drop bombs near the American base. The Japanese hoped American pilots would lose sleep listening to its roar, and not fly as well the next day. When morning came, it was back to the **humid** jungle, mosquitoes, **malaria**, and bad food. Richard missed home, but he welcomed the adventure he hoped would come soon.

In New Guinea, Richard and the other new pilots waited impatiently for orders to fly. Things moved slowly because of

Moresby: morz bee   **humid**: damp and moist   **malaria** (muh **lair** ee uh): a disease carried by mosquitoes

the lack of spare parts, fuel, and **ammunition** for the airplanes. Leaking fuel tanks and damaged parts kept many of the planes in the repair **hangar**. Richard's squadron studied maps and waited for its chance to take on the Japanese. Richard wrote his mother that he spent most of his

World War II mechanics were kept busy repairing damaged planes.

time swimming in the ocean and playing cards. He wanted to know who had won the World Series and what was happening back on the Bong family farm.

ammunition (am yuh **nish** uhn): bullets, bombs, and shells   **hangar**: a large shed for repairing airplanes

Japanese Planes

When World War II began, Allied pilots were not familiar with the Japanese fighters and bombers they fought against in the skies over the Pacific. The pilots soon came up with nicknames for the different planes, because the Japanese names were difficult to pronounce or remember. Japanese fighter planes were given male names such as Tony, Oscar, Jack, and Nick. Japanese bombers received female names such as Betty, Sally, and Lilly. The most well-known Japanese plane was an Imperial Navy fighter called the **Mitsubishi** A6M Zero, nicknamed the Zeke. Like most Japanese planes, the Zero was lightweight and agile, moving like an acrobat in the air. It had little armor to protect it and was built of a light aluminum that allowed pilots to twist and turn easily through the skies. Unfortunately for the Japanese, the Zero also caught fire easily when hit. The Zeke did not have weapons powerful enough to win against newer Allied planes.

IMAGE COURTESY OF THE NATIONAL MUSEUM OF THE U.S. AIR FORCE

Japanese fighter planes were smaller and lighter than American planes.

Mitsubishi: mit su bee shee

Two days after Christmas, Richard got his first taste of air combat. The call came over the base radio that 40 Japanese Zero fighters and 8 Val dive-bombers were heading toward the American base. Richard and 3 other pilots were already flying in the area and were soon joined by 8 more P-38s. Upon sighting the enemy, Captain Thomas **Lynch** dropped his **belly fuel tanks** to make his plane lighter.

A Christmas package from home brings a smile.

He led the attack in a steep dive toward the enemy below. Richard recalled the excitement and fear: "There were Zeroes all over the sky and a flock of dive bombers below them. I tried to remember everything I had ever learned about keeping calm, aiming right, and watching my flight leader. Maybe I was trying too hard—the first four I shot at were a total waste of **lead**. I didn't hit a thing."

Lynch: linch   **belly fuel tank**: outside fuel tank attached to the bottom of the plane that can be dropped when empty
lead (led): the material used in bullets

44

But Richard's luck quickly changed. A Zero closed in on his tail, and he dove sharply to get out of its way. As he skimmed the treetops, a Japanese dive-bomber appeared ahead. "It was a perfect setup even I couldn't miss," he remembered. "I gave him a short burst of bullets and he blew higher than a kite."

Richard had achieved his first air victory, but there was no time to celebrate. He had to keep flying. He pulled up and turned in the opposite

WHI IMAGE ID 11086

Japanese planes sometimes exploded when hit by machine gun fire.

direction. A Zero flew into his line of fire, and Richard fired "an impressive amount of .50 caliber dynamite." The Zero never fired a shot back at him but rolled over on its back and crashed into the ocean. By that time, Richard was nearly out of ammunition. He turned his plane back to base. In his first combat mission, he had shot down 2 enemy planes in less than 10 minutes' time.

Richard's first air battle was a success not just for him but for the whole squadron. Despite being outnumbered, the squadron had destroyed 19 Japanese planes. Not one American plane had been lost. The Japanese had not been prepared for the high-speed dives and **firepower** of the P-38s. Their airplanes could not climb as high as the Americans' and quickly burst into flames when hit by the P-38s' machine guns and cannons.

An "**air ace**" is a pilot with at least 5 planes shot down. It took Richard just 2 weeks of combat to become a member of this **elite** group. On January 7, 1943, Richard's squadron flew with a group of B-17 bombers who planned to attack a **convoy** of Japanese supply ships. During the attack Richard **downed** 2 Zeros. The next day he shot another to bring his total to 5. His friend Tom Lynch was also an ace with 6 victories to his name, so both men were sent to Australia for 2 weeks of **leave**.

Richard was happy to be an ace, but he still missed home. When his mom wrote that his name had appeared in the local newspaper, he replied, "I would much rather be home

---

firepower: ability to use weapons   **air ace**: a pilot with at least 5 planes shot down   **elite** (i leet): special
convoy: group of ships traveling together   **downed**: shot down   **leave**: time off

with no **publicity** whatsoever." Richard was a shy and very private individual. He never enjoyed the fame caused by his flying and avoided attention when he could.

Ships traveled in convoys to protect one another.

In February, Richard was transferred to the Ninth Squadron, 49th Fighter Group stationed at **Schwimmer** Field near Port Moresby. The 49th were known as the "Flying Knights." With Richard's help they became the most successful fighting group in the Pacific. The Flying Knights often attacked convoys of Japanese ships bringing supplies and soldiers to New Guinea. If these supply ships were destroyed, the Japanese troops would not get the food and ammunition they needed to fight. Richard and his squadron took part in several attacks on Japanese convoys in March 1943. Allied aircraft including

publicity (puhb **li** si tee): being noticed by the public in a newspaper or on television   **Schwimmer: shwim** ur

P-38s, B-17 and B-25 bombers, and Australian **Beaufighters** flew out to battle groups of Japanese ships protected by Zeros. Dozens of Japanese ships were sunk as the Zeros tried without success to stop the Allied assault.

At other times the squadron was responsible for protecting their base from attack. On March 11, the Flying Knights were at the camp. That morning, Richard had pitched in a baseball game. Later, he sat playing cards with 3 other pilots. Several others practiced throwing knives at nearby trees or slept in hammocks. Dust blew up from the **airstrip** as a P-38 landed from a patrol mission. Suddenly the phone rang. It was headquarters, reporting that a group of Japanese bombers and their Zero escorts were headed straight for the base. Pilots leapt to their feet, scattering playing cards everywhere as they ran to their planes. Within minutes, the P-38s were airborne and ready for combat.

Soon the squadron spotted the enemy over the ocean. The Japanese bombers flew in low, loaded down with thousands of pounds of explosive bombs meant for the American base at **Dobodura**. Above and to the left flew the Zeros, ready to

Beaufighters: boh fI turz   **airstrip**: runway   **Dobodura**: doh buh **dur** uh

protect the bombers from enemy attack. The Flying Knights flew directly at the bombers. The Zeros dove to meet the attack. Dozens of planes swarmed at each other. Pilots craned their necks to see behind them. The sky filled with bright **tracer bullets** and thick smoke as the first Japanese bomber fell toward the ocean.

Richard spotted a lone Japanese bomber and dove toward it. He hoped to score some hits before being spotted by the bomber's machine gunners. As he started to take aim, 9 Zeros burst from the clouds just behind him. He dove sharply and reached 475 miles per hour before pulling up just above the

ocean's waves. Only one Zero remained on his tail, so he turned and fired at it. The enemy plane exploded and crashed into the ocean.

Tracer bullets lit up the sky and helped pilots find their targets.

tracer bullet: brightly burning ammunition that helps pilots direct fire at the enemy

49

Another swarm of 9 Zeros approached from the left, and Richard turned again to attack. He downed a second plane before diving again. Three Zeros pursued. Their machine guns blazed, and Richard's left engine burst into flames. **Reluctantly**, he turned toward base—but before he could do that, he had to shake off the Zeros. Continuing to dive and turn sharply, he eventually lost his **pursuers** and landed safely. At base, everyone was excited. Richard had survived a close call and managed to down 2 Zeros while outnumbered 9 to 1! Even better, the Flying Knights stopped the Japanese attack on the American base.

This was not the last time Richard would be badly outnumbered and come out ahead. In July, Richard and his flying partner Captain Robert Woods met 8 Japanese Oscar fighters while flying a patrol over New Britain, an island off the coast of New Guinea. Instead of waiting for help, the men decided to attack them head-on. Richard hit one Oscar on the first attack and then came around for a second try. He

reluctantly: not wanting to do something   **pursuer**: person that follows or chases someone in order to catch him or her

downed a second plane before diving toward safety. Several planes followed, and machine gun bullets whizzed past his cockpit as he fought to get away from them.

Richard pushed his plane to its top speed, but his attackers stayed close behind. The Zeros' machine guns let loose again. Bullets ripped into both of Richard's wings and exploded his right tire. His landing gear was badly damaged. Richard fought to maintain control of his P-38. He knew that if he could just make it back to base he had a chance.

Richard continued pushing his plane as fast as it would go. Even badly damaged, his twin-engined P-38 could fly farther than the enemy planes following him. One by one, the Zeros were forced to turn back as they ran low on fuel. Finally, the Schwimmer airstrip came into view. By now, Richard's plane was a smoking wreck. He lowered his wheels with a hand pump and landed just as his P-38 ran out of fuel. Only a pilot like Richard could have survived such a close **encounter** with death.

encounter: an unexpected or difficult meeting

In the autumn of 1943, the Japanese stopped trying to take control of New Guinea and Australia. They were more worried about stopping the Allies and protecting the Japanese homeland. The Japanese hated the idea of enemy planes flying over their country, so their brave soldiers would fight on for 2 more long and bloody years. In the meantime, Richard Bong and his fellow pilots would continue to master their flying skills and to push the Japanese back toward Tokyo.

5

A Reluctant Hero Comes Home

Richard Bong was one of the most talented pilots in the history of the U.S. Army Air Force. He had superior eyesight and often saw enemy planes before his fellow pilots did. He could land on dirt airstrips during storms, fly just a few feet above the trees, and sneak up on an enemy with the sun behind him. Other pilots were better shots, but few were better at getting close behind an enemy before firing. His advice to new pilots was, "Get close and shoot lots of lead." That's exactly what he did.

Another reason Richard was so successful was his complete mastery of the P-38 Lightning. He knew exactly what his plane could do and rarely made a mistake when flying it. In combat, he pushed his plane through dozens of maneuvers that usually put him just where he wanted to be.

Flying Maneuvers

Richard was a highly skilled pilot. He spent hours learning flying maneuvers like the barrel roll, the **chandelle**, and the **Immelmann**. Richard used these and many other tricks when fighting for position against Japanese planes.

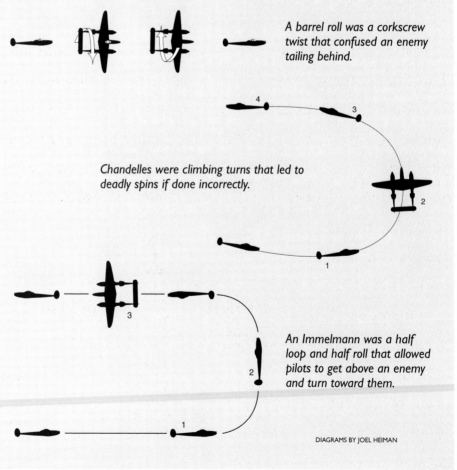

A barrel roll was a corkscrew twist that confused an enemy tailing behind.

Chandelles were climbing turns that led to deadly spins if done incorrectly.

An Immelmann was a half loop and half roll that allowed pilots to get above an enemy and turn toward them.

DIAGRAMS BY JOEL HEIMAN

chandelle: shan **del**   Immelmann: **im** uhl muhn

54

Fortunately for Richard and his fellow pilots, the Americans had several **advantages** over the Japanese. Their planes were tougher and harder to shoot down. American planes had special fuel tanks that did not explode when struck by bullets. They also had more powerful weapons that destroyed the enemy planes with only a few hits.

Just as important, American pilots worked better as a team than the Japanese pilots did. The Japanese flew in 3-plane formations called **shotai**, but once a battle started the formations quickly fell apart, and the pilots often ended up fighting alone. American pilots almost always worked together. Two pairs of planes called a Finger Four flew together and protected each other. Each pair had a leader and a wingman. The wingman flew behind and to the side of his leader to guard against attacks from behind.

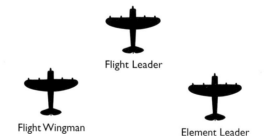

Flight Leader

Flight Wingman

Element Leader

Element Wingman

The Four Finger formation helped American pilots protect one another.

DIAGRAM BY JOEL HEIMAN

advantage: ad **van** tidj   **shotai**: shoh tI

55

The Americans also used radios and **radar** to plan their attacks. Pilots constantly talked to each other and to the flight **coordinator** at their base who kept track of the enemy's movements on the radar screen. The Japanese rarely used radios and so could not communicate with each other once a battle had begun. They also had poor radar systems and were not able to prepare for attacks like the Americans did.

Working at a radar station, this soldier helped locate enemy planes.

By October Richard had 17 "victories," the word used to describe how many planes a pilot had shot down. This was more than any other pilot in the war, a fact that made him famous back home in America. Only Eddie Rickenbacker, who had shot down 26 planes during World War I, had more. Newspaper reporters often asked Richard to talk about his

radar (**ray** dahr): system that detects faraway aircraft by bouncing radio waves off of them
coordinator (koh **ord** uhn ay tur): someone who plans many events to take place around the same time

victories. But Richard didn't really care about beating out his
fellow pilots or about becoming a hero in the United States. He
was a quiet person and preferred spending time with his fellow
pilots rather than talking with reporters. He especially hated
it when reporters called him a "killer." Richard believed he was
doing his job and serving his country and certainly did not
enjoy killing anyone.

What did get Richard excited was the idea of going home.
General Kenney told him he would get a 2-month leave after
his twentieth victory. Richard wrote home to his mother
with the good news. He told her he hoped to be home by the
opening of deer-hunting season in November.

On November 5, Captain Bong downed his twentieth and
twenty-first planes. Just 2 weeks later, Richard was back in the
United States. His first stop was in Washington, D.C., where
he had dinner with General Hap Arnold, chief of the U.S. Army
Air Forces. He enjoyed the fancy meal and the chance to meet
General Arnold, but he wanted to be home. Richard requested
that he be allowed to take the train to Chicago that same night
and was headed toward Poplar early the next morning.

Carl and Dora Bong were very proud of their oldest son.

The Bong family home buzzed with excitement as a crowd waited for their hero's return. Richard's family squeezed together with newspaper reporters, **veterans** from World War I, Richard's college professors, and even 29 members of a local band. Richard's sister Nelda played the piano, and the group sang songs while they waited. At 1:15 a.m., an exhausted Captain Bong arrived. The cheering, hugging, and laughing lasted for more than an hour. Finally everyone went home, and Richard got to sleep in his own bed.

The next few weeks were spent eating his mom's cooking, sleeping late, and catching up with family and friends. Every time Richard entered a restaurant or the Poplar hardware store he was surrounded by people wanting to hear his war stories. He was always polite and cheerful. But he was much

veteran: a person who has fought in a war

Richard's brothers and sisters crowded together to hear his war stories.

more comfortable when it was just his family and closest friends around.

The most annoying part of being a war hero was the newspaper reporters. They constantly called the house and asked the same questions over and over again. They even wrote stories about his family and asked his parents questions about their heroic son.

WHI IMAGE ID 11020

Even a trip to the hardware store drew a crowd for this war hero.

Reporters listened intently when Bong retold another one of his victories.

When hunting season began, the Bong family came up with a trick to keep the reporters away. They knew the newspapers wanted a picture of Richard with a successful kill. Finding and shooting a deer could take many days, and Richard did not want the reporters following him around Poplar's woods. On the first day out, Richard's father shot a large buck. The family pretended Richard had shot the buck, and he posed for pictures as it hung in his yard. The next day the newspapers had their picture of the successful hunter, and Richard and the Bong family had the woods to themselves.

Richard was also asked to crown the king and queen at the homecoming dance at the college he had attended. He did not like to dance or speak in public, but he politely agreed to

Richard pretended he had shot this buck so reporters would leave his family alone.

appear. This was a good decision. At the dance he met a pretty young woman named Marge **Vattendahl**. He had his sister Jerry ask Marge to go on a date with him, and a couple of nights later they went out with Jerry and Richard's friend Pete for dinner and bowling. Marge and Richard got along great. At first she was nervous about being with a famous war hero, but Richard's **humble** nature soon made her feel comfortable. She asked him to tell her about the many medals and ribbons on his uniform, and he replied, "Darned if I know. Someone just pins those things on me from time to time and I keep on wearing them."

Vattendahl: vat uhn dahl   **humble**: not proud

The couple went on many more dates over the rest of Richard's leave. The most memorable was a flight in a **Piper Cub** airplane Richard borrowed from the Superior airport. Richard's mother was also invited along, and the 2 women held hands as Richard turned steeply and flew low over the Bong farm. Marge screamed as the plane passed just over the row of evergreen trees Richard had planted as a boy. Richard sang songs to calm his passengers down and landed safely at the Superior airport.

When he wasn't with Marge or his family, Richard spent most of his 2-month leave performing duties for the military. He spoke at **rallies** where **U.S. war bonds** were sold to raise money for

Richard and Marge enjoyed every minute they spent together.

Piper Cub: small and lightweight passenger plane   **rally**: large meeting   **U.S. war bond**: safe investment sold by the U.S. government

Richard was one of the most talented pilots in the Army Air Force.

was **modest** about his successes. In March he wrote his
mother, "I downed two planes without sticking my neck out
too much." In reality, he and Lynch had attacked 8 aircraft and
narrowly escaped being killed.

Like many American pilots, Bong and Lynch mastered a
few simple rules for defeating the small and agile Japanese
planes.

modest: not thinking too highly of yourself

Rule 1: Stay above the enemy. The P-38 Lightning climbed quickly to high **altitudes**. Bong and Lynch loved to fly high above the clouds, at 20,000 feet or more. There they waited for groups of Japanese planes to approach from below. When the Zero or Oscar pilots least expected it, the P-38 pilots would swoop down on them and scatter the Japanese formation in all directions. If they missed their targets on the first pass, the pilots climbed to get above the enemy and try the same thing again.

Rule 2: Always fly fast. The Japanese airplanes worked best at speeds of 250 miles per hour or below. Any faster, and the Japanese planes could not twist and turn easily. Once the P-38 pilots learned this, they did their best never to let their airspeed go below 300 miles per hour during combat. This meant not spinning and changing direction too much, because fancy maneuvers slowed the planes down. When an enemy was behind them, Bong and Lynch kept their high speeds and tried not to panic. If all else failed, sometimes they turned and flew directly at the enemy. They hoped the P-38s' firepower would win in a head-to-head battle.

altitude: the height of something above the ground

Rule 3: Always pay attention. P-38 pilot Tommy **McGuire** often said, "It is the one you don't see that gets you." During combat, it was easy for pilots to concentrate on the plane they were attacking and forget about the rest of the sky. This was dangerous because unseen enemies could attack at any time. The pilots who survived many combat missions were those who had "eyes in the back of their head." They always knew what was going on around them. Richard Bong was a master of this rule and often saw enemies that other pilots hadn't noticed.

Rule 4: Don't waste ammunition. One of the biggest mistakes made by new pilots was to begin firing at an enemy too early. Hitting a plane moving 300 miles per hour while your plane is moving in a different direction is a nearly impossible task. Many pilots wasted all of their thousands of bullets without even scratching their targets. For Bong and Lynch, the solution was clear: "Get in so close you can't miss and pull the trigger," Richard said.

Unfortunately, bad luck caught up with Lynch after just a month of flying with his friend. Guns from a Japanese ship hit

McGuire: muh **gwIr**

Lynch's plane as he flew over them during an attack. Lynch **ejected** from his plane. But his parachute did not have time to open, and he was killed. Richard's plane was also badly hit. He made it home with 87 bullet holes in his plane. Richard was crushed to lose his friend. Lynch had taught him a great deal about flying, and the 2 men had spent time together in the air and on the ground. He would lose many friends during the war, but few were as important to him as Tom Lynch.

Aces Eddie Rickenbacker and Richard Bong trade stories.

Just a month later, Richard shot down 2 Oscars and broke Rickenbacker's record with his twenty-sixth and twenty-seventh victories. He was now America's "Ace of Aces." He was also **promoted** from captain to major. Reporters followed

ejected: hurled out of the cockpit by a special seat during an emergency   promoted: moved to a higher rank

70

him around his tent for days, taking photographs and asking questions. Richard became so tired of the reporters that he began buzzing low over their tents, usually early in the morning while they were still sleeping. He wrote home to his mother, "I broke the record and by so doing **procured** for myself a lot of trouble."

Bong enjoyed being "Wisconsin Governor for a Day."

The good news was that becoming "Ace of Aces" meant another visit home. Some of the generals were concerned they might lose their new hero if they allowed him to keep flying. Others thought he could help the country even more by traveling around the United States and selling war bonds. Whatever the reasons, Richard was happy to be heading back to Wisconsin, to the family farm, and to Marge.

procured (proh **kyoord**): got something by effort

71

Before he could go home to Poplar, Richard had to fulfill his responsibilities as a famous war hero. He held a **press conference** in Washington, D.C., where he answered the questions he had already been asked so many times before. Richard was bored by the press conference. The only fun part was when Eddie Rickenbacker arrived. Bong and Rickenbacker snuck away from the crowd and sat outside where they could talk alone. Richard loved meeting the World War I ace. The 2 men traded stories, and Rickenbacker

wished Richard good luck during the rest of the war.

The next day Major Bong visited the U.S. Senate. The senators gave him a **standing ovation**, cheering for several minutes. Honored but also embarrassed by all

Bong never enjoyed speaking before crowds even though he had to do it often.

press conference: an interview held by a famous person for reporters   standing ovation: standing up to clap and cheer loudly the attention, he was glad when his duties in Washington were finished and he could get on the train for Chicago.

Captain Bong signs an autograph for a **welder**.

Soon he was back in Poplar with his family and Marge. He could not escape attention for long, but he did find a quiet country road for a special moment with Marge. Richard asked Marge to marry him. She immediately agreed.

The couple had little time to celebrate their engagement. Just a few days later Richard was off to help sell war bonds in 15 states. He flew a P-38 all around the country and gave speeches at dozens of events. Richard met with many flying cadets and gave them advice about how to succeed in the war. He also found time for some fun. While flying in Milwaukee, Richard buzzed right between buildings over busy Milwaukee Avenue. Windows rattled and heads turned as his P-38 roared through downtown and then disappeared over Lake Michigan.

welder: a person who joins pieces of metal or plastic together by heating the pieces until they melt together

Next, America's leading ace next went to Texas for a month-long **gunnery** course. Some pilots would have complained about going back to school to learn how to shoot, but Richard was happy to take the course. He humbly called himself the "lousiest shot in the Army Air Force." During the course, the pilots learned about the latest **techniques** for "**deflection** shooting." This meant shooting ahead of an enemy so he would fly into the stream of bullets. Richard later said he could have greatly increased his number of victories if he had taken the course earlier.

Richard was made a gunnery instructor and sent back to California to teach other pilots how to improve their flying and shooting. Although he was often in the cockpit with his students, he had promised General Kenney he would fly safely and shoot at the enemy only if they shot first. His promise did not last long. Soon he would be involved in some of the fiercest air combat of the entire war.

gunnery: science of operating guns   **technique** (tek **neek**): method or way or doing something that requires skills   **deflection**: making something go in a different direction

7

Home for Good

Staying safe was not easy for Richard Bong. He enjoyed teaching younger pilots about flying, but every time the squadron members went on a mission he itched to go with them. As gunnery instructor he was not supposed to fly in combat. Yet he soon began flying with small groups of planes to check on his pilots' progress. It did not take him long to find trouble.

On October 10, 1944, more than 100 Allied B-17 bombers and 36 P-38 Lightnings attacked **oil refineries** that were under the control of the Japanese at Borneo, an island in the south Pacific. Japanese oil supplies were running low, and the enemy fought fiercely to protect them. As Richard watched from his airplane, 90 Japanese Zeros and Oscars flew out to meet the attack. Tracer bullets filled the skies with flashes of bright light, and Richard decided he could not stay back and

oil refinery (ri fI nur ee): plant where crude oil is turned into gasoline and other types of fuel

watch. He dove toward a pair of Zeros and opened fire with his machine guns.

In just a few minutes, Major Bong downed 2 planes to bring his total to 30. The rest of the attack was just as successful. The oil refineries were badly damaged by the American bombers. Out of the 90 Japanese planes, 61 were destroyed. The Americans lost only one fighter and 4 bombers.

The bad news was that General Kenney was furious with Richard for taking part in the attack. He wanted his star pilot kept safe for the rest of the war. He told his flying ace to stop flying immediately. "Looks like I'm grounded for good this time," Richard wrote Marge. "That ought to make you happy."

But Bong was on the ground for only 2 weeks. It was time for the Allies to push farther north to the Philippines. The Army Air Force would need its best pilots for the job.

The Philippine Islands lie about 2,000 miles south of Japan. Capturing the islands would cut off the Japanese from oil and other supplies in the East Indies. For much of the twentieth century, the Philippines had been under the control

of the United States. But the U.S. abandoned the islands in
1942. That's when Japan gained control of the Philippines
in a fierce battle with General MacArthur. Thousands of
captured Americans had died when Japanese soldiers forced
the prisoners to walk nearly 90 miles to a prison camp. That
horrible march became known as the **Bataan** Death March.
But General MacArthur had stated, "I shall return." Now it was
time for the Americans to keep that promise.

General MacArthur returned to the Philippines as he had promised in
October 1944.

Bataan: buh **tahn**

Soldiers of the U.S. Sixth Army landed on the Philippine island of **Leyte** on October 20. They quickly began building runways for the Army Air Force. One week later, 34 P-38s landed at the newly constructed air base. Richard Bong was one of the first pilots to hop out of his plane at Leyte. General Kenney and General MacArthur were both there to greet him. Japanese troops arrived by the thousands to fight off the American advance, and Richard led one of the first patrols of the area. He shot down a Zero to bring his total to 31.

Life in Leyte was horrible. It rained every day. The camp quickly became a swamp. Japanese planes flew over the base at night,

WHI IMAGE ID 11368

World War II airstrips were often nothing more than open fields carved out of the jungle, like this one at **Iwo Jima**.

dropping bombs and making sleep nearly impossible. Richard wrote his mother that nighttime was "just like the 4th of July, bright lights and lots of noise all night long." Flying was even

Leyte: lay tee   **Iwo Jima:** ee woh jee mah

more dangerous. The airstrips were wet and poorly made. The planes skidded when landing or slid off into the jungle when pilots lost control.

But Richard was happy to be back in action. On his second day, he flew with 3 other P-38s on a patrol mission around the island. As the planes headed for home, he spotted 17 Oscars preparing to attack the base. Without **hesitating**, Richard dove and fired into the formation. The Oscars scattered and then turned to come after the Americans. Badly outnumbered, the P-38 pilots fought furiously. They chased the attackers away and protected their base. Richard shot down 2 Oscars and damaged 2 others before being hit himself. With one engine dead, he turned toward base and landed safely.

The excitement continued the next day. After completing another patrol, Richard landed just as 3 Japanese Val bombers flew over the runway. The bombers opened up with machine guns and dropped bombs in all directions. Richard was not afraid. He calmly drove down the runway and jumped out of his plane as bombs kept falling. The crew chief yelled at him

hesitating: pausing before doing something

to hide under the P-38's wing, but Bong walked off the runway without even looking up.

With 33 victories, few pilots dreamed of taking away Richard's title "Ace of Aces." Only one serious **rival** remained. Major Tommy McGuire wanted to beat out Richard and become the top American pilot. McGuire was commander of the 431st Squadron and constantly flew the skies above the Philippines in his P-38 looking for Japanese planes.

Major Tommy McGuire badly wanted Bong's title "Ace of Aces."

Bong and McGuire were complete opposites. Richard was quiet and modest. McGuire was loud and **aggressive**. Richard was round faced and handsome. McGuire was thin and awkward looking. Richard rarely talked about his victories, while McGuire bragged about his superior

rival (**rI** vuhl): person competing against someone   aggressive (uh **gre** siv): fierce or threatening flying abilities. The 2 men had just one thing in common: they were both amazing pilots.

Bong and McGuire shot down Japanese planes at an excellent rate. In less than 2 months Bong destroyed 4 Zeros, 4 Oscars, a Sally bomber, and a Tojo fighter. During that same period, McGuire downed 3 Zeros, 3 Tojos, an Oscar, and 2 Jack fighters. By December Bong had 38 total victories, and McGuire had 30.

This ace race was interrupted by a visit from General Douglas MacArthur to the Leyte airfield on December 12. MacArthur presented Richard with America's highest military award, the **Congressional** Medal of Honor. The general had prepared a speech,

General MacArthur presented Major Bong with the Congressional Medal of Honor.

Congressional (kuhn **gre** shuhn uhl): having tò do with Congress

81

but at the last minute he decided to speak from his heart instead. He said, "Major Richard Bong, who has ruled the air from New Guinea to the Philippines, I now **induct** you into the society of the bravest of the brave, the wearers of the Congressional Medal of Honor."

Only 15 pilots were awarded the Congressional Medal of Honor during World War II.

Richard was grateful to receive such a rare honor but also glad when the ceremony ended and people stopped staring at him. After MacArthur left, he stuck the medal in his pocket and went to the mess tent for a tuna sandwich. That was the last anyone on base heard from Richard about winning such a medal. He rarely mentioned the Congressional Medal of Honor or his many other awards. He preferred to be just one among many pilots.

induct: to let into an elite group

General Kenney decided to send Major Bong home for good as soon as the pilot reached 40 victories. This did not take long. Richard shot down an Oscar on December 15 and another Oscar the next day. He wanted to keep flying, but General Kenney told him it was time to go home and marry his girl. After a final visit with members of his squadron, Richard climbed aboard an army plane and headed back to the United States.

Richard had flown 146 combat missions and been in combat for more than 400 hours. He was known across the United States as one of the greatest pilots in American history. His record of 40 victories would not be broken, though his friend Tommy McGuire got close. McGuire made it to 38 victories before losing control of his plane and crashing to his death in early January. By that time Richard was safely back in Wisconsin, preparing for his wedding.

Richard and Marge wanted to get married and start their new lives together as soon as possible. They hoped to have a small wedding for family and close friends. This was not to happen. So many people had been kind to Richard and Marge during the war that their invitation list grew every day. Almost 1,300 people crammed the church in Superior on the big day in early February. Another 600 people without invitations waited outside in the freezing cold, hoping for a glimpse of the famous pilot and his bride.

Richard and Marge were married in February of 1945.

No cameras were allowed inside the church during the actual wedding, so Richard and Marge had to act out the ceremony a second time for cameramen later that night. The wedding was shown on news programs all across the country. They even taped Richard and Marge cutting their huge wedding cake. The cake was 7 feet long and was made with 1,000 eggs, 175 pounds of flour, and 16 gallons of milk!

Late that night the couple escaped all of the excitement and headed west to California for their honeymoon. Richard took Marge for her first flight in a P-38 while visiting an air base in Los Angeles. They went snowshoeing in **Sequoia** National Park and met more **celebrities** in Hollywood. Richard and Marge had a great time wherever they went. They were glad to be together at last.

Richard sang to Marge during her first flight in a P-38 Lightning.

Richard and Marge's honeymoon went by in a flash. Before they knew it, it was time for Richard to get back to work.

Sequoia: si **koi** uh   **celebrity** (suh **leb** ri tee): a famous person, especially an entertainer or a movie star

But this time, leaving home would be different. Marge would be with him. After a short training period at Wright Air Force Base in Dayton, Ohio, Richard was sent back to California to fly planes for the Lockheed airplane company. Lockheed was working on a new **jet engine** plane called the P-80 Shooting Star. The company wanted Richard to test the plane for them.

The P-80 Shooting Star was America's first jet fighter.

The Germans had designed a jet-powered plane called the **Messerschmitt** 262 that was faster than any small plane in the sky. Few of these German jets had been built, but the U.S. Army Air Force badly wanted its

The German Messerschmitt 262 was the first jet airplane used in combat.

jet engine: engine that creates power by pushing hot gases behind the plane   **Messerschmitt**: mes ur shmit

own jet plane to compete with the "Me 262." They believed
the Shooting Star was the answer. The army hoped that the
P-80 would be ready as quickly as possible.

Flying a brand-new airplane was dangerous. Lockheed
engineers experimented with many versions of the jet engine,
but all of them had problems. The biggest problem was
that the engine sometimes died soon after takeoff. Several
pilots had already lost their lives testing the P-80 by the time
Richard started flying them in July.

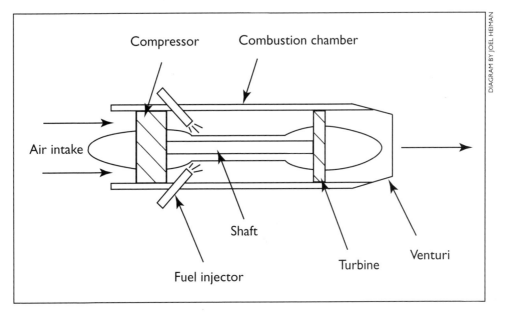

Diagram of a jet engine.

But Richard was not afraid. He had survived many close calls over New Guinea and the Philippines. He believed his flying skills were good enough that he could survive almost any emergency in the air. He flew the Shooting Star 12 times during his first month and had few problems. He and Marge were quickly settling in to life in Hollywood. Marge took up painting, and Richard played golf when he was not flying. And there was good news about the war. In June, the Allies declared victory in Europe. If the war in the Pacific was won, World War II would be over.

On August 5, Richard and Marge went to dinner with a group of friends. The couple left the restaurant early so Richard could get some sleep before another week of flying. It was the last time they would have dinner together.

The next morning, Richard climbed into his P-80 for another test flight. He almost canceled the flight so he could play golf with the celebrity Bing Crosby. But Richard forgot his golf shoes at home and decided to fly instead. His plane took off normally. When it reached 400 feet above the ground, however, a puff of black smoke poured from the

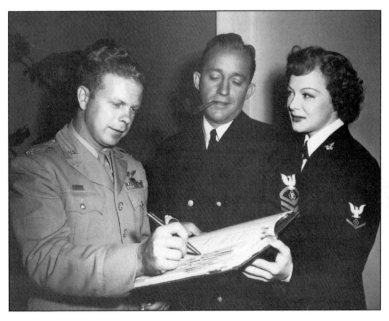

Richard signs an autograph for Bing Crosby.

plane's tailpipe. The engine flamed out, and the plane began diving toward the ground.

Richard kept his cool as he had during so many emergency landings during the war. He knew he could not immediately abandon the plane. There were hundreds of houses below him. If he ejected from the plane, it would certainly smash into a house and probably kill innocent people. So Richard steered the P-80 toward an empty lot, hoping the plane would

89

crash safely away from the surrounding homes. At the last second, he opened the cockpit and flew out into the air.

Richard's parachute sprung open, but it was too late. The plane was just a few hundred feet above the ground. The parachute did not have time to fully inflate. Richard was killed instantly when his body hit the ground 100 feet from the exploded plane.

Marge and the Bong family were **devastated** by the news. Richard had survived so many dangerous battles with the Japanese, and now had been killed within sight of his new California home. Marge and Richard had enjoyed marriage for just 6 months before the tragic accident. How had something so terrible happened to such a wonderful man?

The next morning the nation read about Bong's death in all of the major newspapers. But another significant news item was printed that day. On the other side of the world, an airplane named the *Enola Gay* had dropped the first **atomic bomb** on the Japanese city of **Hiroshima**. It was the most powerful weapon ever used by humans. More than

devastated: shocked or distressed   **atomic** (uh **tom** ik) **bomb**: a powerful bomb that explodes with great force, heat, and light, enough to destroy large areas   **Hiroshima**: hi **roh** shuh muh

In Milwaukee, Major Bong's death was even bigger news than the atom bomb.

70,000 Japanese citizens were instantly killed. This bomb and another dropped on **Nagasaki** 3 days later would finally bring an end to the war in the Pacific as well as an end to World War II.

Nagasaki: nah gah **sah** kee

Despite the importance of the first atomic bomb, Richard's death was the top story that day. The *Los Angeles Times* front page read, "MAJOR BONG KILLED!" Below that, in smaller print, the attack on Hiroshima was described. It wasn't that the atomic bomb was less important. It was that Richard Bong was America's war hero, loved

No one could imagine the death and damage caused by the atomic bomb.

by everyone. His death was a shock to the nation. People across the country sent messages and sympathy cards to Marge and the Bong family.

Richard's funeral was held in Poplar a few days later. Thousands of people stood along the route to Poplar as his funeral car slowly rolled toward the cemetery. Eighteen P-47 Thunderbolts flew overhead and dipped their wings in airmen salute as the coffin was lowered into the ground.

After the funeral, Marge stayed in California. Eventually, she married again. She had 2 daughters and a happy family life, but she never forgot her first love. She returned to Wisconsin in 1985

Marge and General Kenney attended this remembrance of Richard's life.

when the Richard I. Bong Memorial Bridge was built. She became close with the Bong family again and began spending more time in Poplar. Soon she started working with Bong's brothers and sisters to raise money for a museum dedicated to Richard and other World War II veterans. The Richard I. Bong Veterans Historical Center opened in 2002. It welcomes thousands of visitors every year. It is a fitting way to honor a true American hero and a wonderful place to learn about the many men and women who gave their lives during a long and brutal war.

93

The Richard I. Bong Veterans Historical Center in Superior opened in September 2002.

The Richard I. Bong Memorial Bridge connects Superior, Wisconsin, to Duluth, Minnesota.